THE GUIDMAN'S DAUGHTER

THE GUIDMAN'S DAUGHTER

HENRY MARSH

2009

For the woman in blue

Maclean Dubois

Also by Henry Marsh

A *First Sighting*, ISBN 0-9514470-1-7
first published 2005
Maclean Dubois,
Hillend House, Hillend,
Edinburgh EH10 7DX

A *Turbulent Wake*, ISBN 978-0-9514470-4-8
first published 2007
Maclean Dubois

A *Trail of Dreaming*, ISBN 13-978-0-9561141-0-5
in collaboration with the artist, Kym Needle,
published 2009
Open Eye Gallery,
34 Abercromby Place,
Edinburgh EH3 6QE

Printed by Cromwell Press Group, www.cromwellpress.co.uk
Design by Cate Stewart
Distributed by Birlinn Ltd

Acknowledgements

I am grateful to the editors of *Northwords Now* and *Dream Catcher* where some of these poems were first published.

Much of the detail in the twelve poems on Mary, Queen of Scots – *The Guidman's Daughter* – I owe to John Guy's biography, *My Heart is my Own*. I asked Professor Guy if he would look over my poems to check that there were no obvious howlers - and he very kindly did so. I must also thank Dr Rosalind Marshall for her perspicacious comments on the Introduction. George Harris also offered helpful advice. I owe them all a great debt of gratitude. Four of the poems from the *Guidman's Daughter* first appeared in *Poetry for a Queen*, a booklet published by the Marie Stuart Society.

Peter Gilmour has provided great help and most useful advice in the selection and arrangement of the collection. Many thanks also to Kym Needle who produced the drawing for the cover. As ever, Professor Alexander McCall Smith and his team have been unfailing in their support and encouragement. Without him, this venture would not have been possible.
Thank you.

THE GUIDMAN'S DAUGHTER

I

Sea Campion

A day without you is uncreated.
I pass the time, get lost
in this and that, return to a scene
unseasonably dreich. The trees
are roused from summer silence, restive
in an east wind. Torn leaves,
gummed to the wet road, are bitter
scented. I remember a gully in a cliff
where the same unreasonable wind
set the North Sea sucking
and grinding its teeth. On a rock slab
a tumble of white silene
glittered in the rain, its tossing bells
ringing in the eye. I reach you through
this carillon and turn content
to the tasks of a redeemed day.

Out of the Dark

Winter is a weight on the sea.
Stars are falling into the breathing surf.
Orion is aloof and stubborn,
studded to a bleak bulkhead.
Warmth seduces. Fire flames
ghost across closed eye-lids.
Cheeks burn – backs
freeze. Sleep drags
to the tomb of a bedroom. Bored
with lucidity, the window enjoys
the night in transmission – the cold
unfolds in opaque equations.

Morning elms are hoarse –
have found their voice. Etched
flat on a slate sky,
navigation through the net seems
improbable. But rooks are
bouncing and dancing, steering
between suppliant limbs,
assuring that the sap will rise –
unfold its pulse in the sun.
They wheel in sudden clamour,
settle to talk the wisdom
of a black brooding on icy sticks.

Why remember only now, shadows
of birds, lustre on the night sea?
Slowly, roots are finding the dark.
And yesterday, I found a grief
that unreality had shrouded.
After forty years it broke
through a window in a film.

And meeting – knowing, utterly,
that love would grow, your gifts
of body and spirit, your quiet,
insistent goodness lead into life.
All this, beyond my agency.

Machair Flowers

Eye-bright,
bedstraw,
pink, fragrant
orchid,
a field of barley –
these are the summer gifts
you bring to our life.

As for my
contribution –
awkward bramble,
the arrogant thistle,
and the frog
orchid,
that refuses to change
to a prince.

January Morning

As a traveller excited by a strange land
returns to his world now made
mysterious by his liberation, I pass
through the gate of waking to the light
of a dawn – perhaps a dream hovering
out of sleep – that fires the embers
of a cloud-cave roof, sets
charred sticks of trees searching
into powder-blue and gold, brings
the bronze of the hill's shoulder,
the masterly studies in puddles, dancing
to the eye. The moon is straining
its pale ear to catch the first
song of a distant mistle thrush.

Oh the words, the words. You'd be
embarrassed if I said I find you there.
But being familiar with this threshold,
you can follow to the brink and catch
the wordless benediction in the morning.
Then what is shared can speak for us.

Archetype

Perugia

The girl
in a blue dress
who smells like rain,
a sharp shower
drying
on a warm country road –
a bright blue
but unassertive,
like the small
butterfly,
the delicate
harebell

or a glimpse
of Poussin's skies,
the source of light
behind
his calculated clouds –
becomes

the woman
in blue
with stars at her head,
like the mother
with the burden
on her knees,
slim hands crossed,
eyes lost
in another's sorrow,
searching out a way,
stubborn
only in charity.

Wind Song

Take from this wind the songs
of scarred rocks, shot silks
of fine rain and sun-burst
revelations, the folding
agitation of yellow flags
and buttercups in nodding, curt,
acknowledgement of what passes,
three grey ponies bowed
under the spume of their manes
and charged crests running
the spine of the Atlantic horizon.

Then at dawn, through the whoom
and whine, the wind's polyphony,
I wake at a cuckoo shout and see
the yellow dancers, their bend
and flow, that stubborn, fleeting
resilience. And turn to what I have,
our moments in this turbulence. Hear
the delicate breath of your sleeping
and think of all I never say.
For I am like the wind's damage –
but dumb to sing a simple yes.

II

A Young Girl with Daisies

Some dealer
no doubt, found the name,
the shrewd glance
quick in an appraisal
that saw no need
to linger
on the flowers.

Bonny,
not beautiful,
she holds, perhaps,
not daisies
but Camomile,
Milkwort,
Convolvulus
and what will become
the Flander's Poppy.

Why the pedantry?
Because,
Renoir knows
the flush of the blood
alight
beneath the skin,
is too precious
for
inexactitude,
and what she holds
in her hands
withers
even as he paints.

The Virgin and Child with St John the Baptist and an Unidentified Saint

Titian

The scene is pastoral, seemingly tranquil.
St John has placed his right hand
on the shoulders of a lamb – a fatherly,
loving restraint. His left hand points
to the mystery he is reading in a beast.
He seems lost in thought.

The Virgin has turned from her child,
her gaze directed at what has become
the Lamb. Jesus has twisted in her arms.
He stretches for the unknown Saint
in the way infants do
for someone loving and familiar.

Nothing deflects the wordless passage
between her and John. It's as if
she suddenly sees what nothing
can prepare her for: the impossible paradox –
Divine mortality. It has no comfort for her.
She knows that lambs are for slaughter.

Bosch found Christ's tormentors
in his streets. And Titian's John –
so obviously a young Italian.
The Virgin is in pink Venetian silk.
Yet her blue connects
to a distant land and the infinite sky.

The Three Ages of Man

Titian

He's adrift in her eyes – a romantic.
Her gaze is a little harder. As if
she wanted a decision. They have lost
interest in making music – their song
is singing them.

It hardly needs Cupid dancing
on the infants under his feet.
He could be treading grapes
in canny preparation
for his next vintage.

The clouds are mellow. But high
above the lovers' heads, flung
wisps of mare's tails
are entering the picture. Conclusions
are in the air.

In evening sunlight the church is
insubstantial. Is our destination
assured? A tide is rising –
soon, shadow will flood
the landscape.

An old fellow is sitting
by a shattered stump. Wherever
he looks his eyes are filled
with loss. He is pretending
to be wise.

He has made masks
from a couple of pumpkins.

Man in Armour

Rembrandt

It hardly seems his armour, the helmet
too weighty for the fine young head,
the lance and shield washed up
from a by-gone age. Or perhaps
Rembrandt couldn't compromise, driven
by a tyrannical eye that refused to stretch
his model to an archaic tilt-yard bruiser.

Perhaps it was the armour's spell – gleams
out of his favoured gloom, the palpable
weight. The lad just carried the gear.
Straps and buckles, joints, the meticulously
worked metal, offered the seduction
of technical mastery, its power by proxy
transposing to a masterly rendering in paint.

Or was it a commissioned Dutch display –
like gold or tulips – a justification through
faith in possessions, that itch of incipient
wealth doomed to proclaim itself in gestures
that never quite fit? So someone
had hired the expensive mould that, broken
open, would never disclose a warrior.

A Summer Day – Carnoustie

After William McTaggart

A song of light and sea finds voice
in fisher-girls, translucent
on the more substantial water.
They wade with laden creels
from boats moored to a reef.
Even their fish are ghosted, tricks
of light they heap on wet rocks.

Her load strapped to head and back,
a black-shawled fishwife
would call at the door, her cheeks
like withered apples, her eyes
blue-grey in their watery distance.
The creamy haddock draped
across my palms, I'd hurry to the larder.

No boats – though an oil-rig
is painfully nudging towards
Dundee. The army is racketing
at Barry Buddon. Carnoustie prospers
on the thwack of golf clubs.
But you catch his light. It resolves
to the cooling metal of distant Fife.

After Edward Hopper

Winter-bleached, the grass
is ochre across the undulations
of the wasteland. Its hogweed
has been welded from bits of pipe
and showerheads. Perhaps it's landed
from another planet. It stands
along the skyline, makes a black
fence against the white walls
of a factory shed. The roof
is black. A chimney, black and thin
as a telephone pole, has unfurled
a banner of white smoke. It hangs,
unmoving, across pale blue.
Nothing stirs. The scene
is urgent with unease. Something,
somewhere, might be malignant.

The stillness is the gesture of a cry
trapped in the palest amber
of a winter afternoon. Then
you see that a skein of geese
or jaunty magpie would crack
the spell, drag life across
the frame of our bleak damage.

From Courthill House, Inverkeilor

For Kym and Kristien Needle

The bay under this white house spreads
like a slow smile. October light
walks on water. Its prints are cool
scalds that burn in vaporous silver.

From keels carried on bitter winds,
berserkers launched here. The gorged
crows were loud over Corbie Knowe.

Only a solitary gull and an afternoon breeze
patrol the red-stained sand.

As dusk closes, the room glows
like the heart of a cinder. Seeds of Dreamtime
smoulder on the walls. Gum trees
breath their blue distance, draw
the spirit from comfortable moorings.
A farmhouse squats in solitary, angular
denial, while the sacred flows in leaf
and rock, threatening inundation.

Out in the bristling dark, we know
joy in the trace of the starlight serpent.

Lemon as a gull's eye, dawn opens
our window, inflames to outback-orange.
A black bird shifts, jagged,
through a black tree. No song
in October – but the tree is twisted
in some desperate effort of articulation.

Reaching through our sleepy room, light
touches the bottom corner of a canvas.
Another dawn is seeping through orange,
sets dancing other gesticulating trees,
engenders the blue-gum haze. Dream-
time is passing into the Dreamtime.

III

From the Airwaves

The song opens on a rusty hinge.
It resonates in a wave-vaulted
nave. Each note is placed
in a phrase at a distance too
great for the febrile human
memory to conceive as music.

In ocean glooms the Leviathan
finds itself through choral
constellations that map its own
unfathomable space
and time. The great head
resounds in cadences of knowing.

An old tramp steamer, freighted
with child slaves, is somewhere
off the coast of Benin.
The radio suggests that the Captain,
now that the game is up,
is throwing them over the side.

Staring-eyed, caught in apparently
weightless choreography,
they spin slowly through the deeps,
their angled limbs and expectant
palms in open supplication,
deaf to the sea's chorale.

Two-faced

Whump. Every few minutes
it kicks the house. The old chimney
moans by the bed as the ghostly boot
goes in. Tonight, the eye
in the vortex is dangerously depressed.
It takes a saturnine satisfaction
in the scouring abrasions of its rain.
It thinks in squalls, exults
in the searing voltage of its under-life
belied by the drifting duck-down
of its other, moonlit face.

Star-side up, there is deceptive
serenity. Where the fleece tears
the moon peers down its racing
spotlights, catches in pale
pools luminous nematodes
shuttling to orange galaxies
where they scatter like startled fish.
It hears, carried on updrafts,
the ceaseless babble that wraps
the planet, the exchange of inanities
and possibly terminal delusions.

At times it gathers practical advice:
He cannae keep them in his troosers
so he shoves his fags doon his pants
tae keep them frae the bluddy junkies.

No wonder the wind is desperate.

The Launch

The shed festooned – spiders assiduous
in the entrapment of dust. Damp
has mapped across the roof, rusted
wrenches and screw-drivers, a drip
has puddled on an old car battery.
The sun strains through the spotted window,
lights the planetary motes. I haven't seen
the garden syringe for a while, he says.

Should I tell him? Fifty years before
we'd made a rocket, set it on the beach
in the syringe launcher. The blast
rocked gulls, sent ladies
to their sea-front windows expecting
the second maroon. A white cloud
drifted nonchalantly along the rocks.
Envious of the daffodils, the brass tube
had unfolded in exotic petals. Fragments
of rocket cart-wheeled into the sea.
Years later I saw our chief technician
on 'The Sky at Night'. Apparently intact.

Advent

Past a low sun
a score of gulls
is plying
north east. At each
beat, their grey wings
dip
and glitter in gold

hinting
that what is invisible might
be accessible.

So pure water frets
in silver,
stars condense
from darkness
and the winged ones
took form
from caller air.

Persephone

For Alice – January 20th

He felt the pluck, they say, as she gathered flowers –
transmission through the outraged root?
A delicate, tendril-signal connecting
through an unimaginable dark? And himself,
like a morbid spider at the unspeakable centre
with little else to think about but a hapless
girl's joyous transgression. Then how
did he cope with the slicing pain of harvest?
Soothed himself in winter, took time
for sullen restoration? Tested his wounds
knowing there were powers he wouldn't contain?

So back through the earth she crowds,
spreading with the light across the planet –
her perpetual circuit of renewal.
And just at the moment I remembered to look
I met her – an unlikely arrival
from under a naked hedge, with nothing
triumphal in the sodden detritus but a garland
of rusty wire – a lucid, pendent
pearl – girl with an ear-ring –
in a cluster of white-spiked buds
turgid with the freedom of her resurrection.

And beyond the snowdrops in the lane,
beyond the immaculate swans on the canal
mirrored in their perfect choreography
of mating, are eyes, still dark
from their underworld, hardly adjusted
to the miraculous light – a child born
with hints of spring. As if for the first time,
I see a human face, trace
the strange, intricate whorl of an ear
lucent as the nacre of a pink shell –
and know a pearl would be distraction.

At Rosslyn Chapel

A child sitting on a Knight's tombstone –
you wonder if his bones are there.
She kicks her heels. Suppose he roused
at the indignity, his Red Cross burning?

No horses, hounds nor sword,
no Sancho Panza – a solitary, ghostly
manual of redundant skills and babbling
in medieval Scots a story of Jerusalem.

Some claim that childhood was recently
invented – a scholar's tale? But just one
glimpse through the rust-frozen visor
and time would collapse. He'd be disarmed.

And should he make outside, the weight
of armorial junk thrown off,
he'd see what really signifies is a script
in the air, the arabesques of jaunty swallows.

If he read the child and passing birds
the shortness of our time could crush,
our centuries of darkness. But he'd take
his lute and sing the beauty of continuity.

By Jock's Road

If you were to doze here, you might
have a strange awakening. In the strewn,
glacial wreckage, the rowans are grey
as the rocks, the birches rooted
in fissures. Over Craig Maude,
ravens are talking. They give voice
to the script hidden in the rune trees.

It cannot be translated. And whatever
the wind's message, it mumbles behind
the threshold of articulation. The place,
you feel, is charged, eerie
with the unspoken. Even at noon,
the wood seems twilit. What souls
are struggling in these twisted trees?

Suddenly you walk free. Brassy
as the unequivocal sun, along the Dounalt
peregrines are screaming invective, stooping
at a casual eagle. Spring – but the river
is tamed by drought. Winter grasses
glitter. Roused butterflies twist
and flirt – but primroses are a life away.

Summer – arrived with a shout. You remember
the faltering steps of our shy Aprils,
sheltering behind dykes, the textures
of the veils of rain – the seduction of slow
disclosure. We're dulled by easy stimuli.
Swallows are early at the farm, drawn
by the ebb of old, protracted mysteries.

Darwin's Cathedral

Remembering the Mata Atlântica

A dreich day – New Town
stone is dark with rain. The railings
round Moray Gardens glisten,
May leaves droop. A heavy wind
is shaking their prodigal drops. Eyes
are dark under twisting umbrellas. Xango
echoes in my head, a memory of drums.

Storms roll along the mountains –
his purgatorial fire. Coiled under thunder,
the viper – a wisdom that might kill.
From a spur we map the forest's scars,
climb round a landslide. And Indians?
Cannibals, they say – long gone.
But we touch on what they knew.

For the forest survives the buzz-saw
of the cicada. Ants urge past under sails
of leaves. Purple tibouchina flaunts
in the rolling canopy. Reichsteinaria
cascades, scarlet, to a turbulent river
where blue bolts of butterflies flap
and stagger with their weight of voltage.

A thumb-nail toad, gold-stars
a glassy leaf from a hanging garden.
Candle-flame flowers light a passage
through gloom to a vaulted nave
stained by traceries of sun and orchids.
Xango echoes in my head – he throbs
in the pulse of the song of the one voice.

Exposure

The recycling lorry came at noon.
That evening, we took a walk
under the swallows. And down
the road I found two poems
under a hawthorn hedge –
a third was stretched and martyred.
Exposed – caught *in flagrante*.
And the beeches whispering.

But a car sped by,
a girl on a bike. And a beetle
scaled across the words – who
couldn't read. What strange
intrusion into its world – a pale,
flat flower hanging
in the blossom, bereft of nectar.
I shoved the pages into my pocket.

So why the fuss? Unlikely
that the bloke on the lorry would stop
to read – and what's a bit of litter?
And why, after all, do I write?
They're hardly Sibyl's leaves.
I wonder, though, what she thought
as she watched her more wayward
words settling into mulch.

Renewal

A tall old man came to do the hedge.
Skeletal, I feared he would unhinge
and clatter down the ladder. The face
was small and wizened, dabbed
with patches of steel-wool hair.
Under high summer his nails were blue.

Timidly, he tilted at the privet, exposed
some hidden holes and caves, retired
for a flask of tea, then an early lunch;
took refuge from a shower, worried
that the electric trimmer might impart
a surge of unmanageable energy.

After two hours, in kindness to the hedge,
I paid him. And when he'd gone
in his wheezing van, I finished it myself.
Retired, he'd said, but needed the money
for his ailing wife. The hedge recovered.
But somewhere, perhaps, is a lost man.

Canal in Autumn - Maryhill

Wintry breaths – a thin
mist is polishing the glass.
But the light, restrained,
muted, sees further.
It permits you to enter. Alders
drown in brown. From endless,
lucid depths a birch
grows upwards from its twigs,
their few, sunk leaves
like uncertain glimmers of fish
or fragments fallen
from the morning moon.
The reflection elbows
at the root in a watery
metamorphosis, becomes
substantial in the air – enough
to carry a few small
birds and the frail sun.
Though a ripple threatens,
the image is persistent – it follows
as you pass till swallowed
behind by the gulp of a bridge.

By Bilston

Sites of the Battle of Rosslyn 1303

A scarred land, scrub land.
   Whun-staned stockyards
are surrendering to bone-pale
   saplings. The birches thresh
in moody descant to the theme
   of a winter wind. In waves
it throws itself on whins – pikemen
   resolute above Shinbanes Fields.
Their flowers are sparse. In palms
   of petals they hold their sex
like carefully nurtured flames.
   Grey stones and twilight names:
Kill Burn, Hewan bog.
   And the flicker of January flowers.

They suck at your feet – the dead.
   And slipping in the mud transmits
their message through the bone:
   a starling-flock of arrows singing
into battle; the shock, the push –
   a slope falling away – earth
opening for their delivery; a burn
   in bloody spate; night
groaning into the dawn's silence;
   rags of darkness condensing
into flocks of crows. And a few
   knew, that once, on a day,
they'd lived an unspeakable joy
   that only comrades understood.

You wait – perhaps hope –
    for something to cry out.
Interpret carefully the cadences
    of wind and tree. But their song
is indifferent, might be anywhere.
    Did folk remember the stench,
death quickening the earth
    in Shinbanes Field, at least,
for a few summers? A flurry
    of sleet spatters rings
on a puddle. They merge in chaotic
    patterns, sink away. Leave
pale, uneasy reflections
    of a few small flowers.

McPherson's Rant – Banff, 1700

For Ian Laing

November murk – and a rope
swinging. As they clear the stalls
from a windy market and their feet
from slurry, a tune unfolds
by the gallows, winds into the mind.

While eyes are marvelling
at dancing fingers, time
stops. But the town clock
moves. Stealthy, at first –
to dream-fast. For he sees a danger
of reprieve – the Sheriff's man.
He steals an hour. And a song
that might last forever,
its variations conjured by demonic
fingers, falls silent.

And the felon player, lost
like a waking child, looks round,
offers the crowd his fiddle.

They fear possession, bewitchment
by music. They hang, poised
in the moment, their blood too
thin for temptation. He watches
the eyes shift – who'll break
from the flock? And suddenly,
he understands his freedom,
laughs as he smashes his violin.

They thraw his neck. But
his tune is wandering the alleys
of their souls, passes across
November darkness to immortality.

On the Glasgow Train

She sits opposite. Wrings her hands
round her mobile. Her head, pushed
back into her seat shifts, side
to side. She settles.

Yawns. The blue-grey eyes
fix. But their broken panes
will not allow her passage
to the dreich fields.

Flares in the murk over Grangemouth
appear to make her shiver. Her phone
won't work. I don't have mine to give.
She wears two brooches:

on one lapel of her grey suit,
a poppy; the other carries the photo
of a soldier. They share the shape of a mouth,
the arch of an eye-brow.

You're in distress, my wife says.
I bless her for speaking. The son
was killed by a roadside bomb. November
is a difficult month.

Unemployed – he went for a soldier.
Eighteen years – three weeks in Iraq.
The black puddles in a derelict yard
could be fathomless.

To die for a lie. I remember, though,
a September in Central Park
and a woman, her coat rain-black,
weeping for her children.

IV

Apples

Giovanna Garzoni paints,
in a still life, her apples
with blemishes. You smell them,
feel the scratch of their brittle
autumn leaves. Did she know
Galileo Galilei? He studies

the spots on the face of the sun –
overturns the applecart.
What price the passionate,
unconditional eye? Emily
has seen her first apple –
on a tree. She manages the word.

But apples should be waxed
and shiny. Doubtful, like meeting
a strange child, she reaches
to touch the stained cheek.
And plucks. She hands it to me.
'Ta,' she says. She'll learn.

Then we gather raspberries.
A late variety – yes – but
in November? The grass, it seems,
is in a May surge. What
will we bequeath? A wind
is rising. We hurry to shelter.

By Loch Long

Not so much a gully – more
a fissure in the rock, its faces trickling
into rushing gloom. Ferns hang
from perilous foot-holds, thin trees.
At the top, paths cross in a thicket
by a headless lamp-post – startled,
you expect Mr Tumnus to hustle by.

And the villa with its Italian tower –
abandoned, overgrown, just held
at the brink of oblivion. Its weight
of wisteria might drag it there. You see
through murky windows a drawing room,
the carpet in the madder of spent roses,
pictures and furniture surprisingly intact.

For her it seems an adventure – caught
in a story-book wood where space
has closed in winding green tunnels,
where bumbling ogres lurk under bridges.
'Come on grandpa,' she says. 'Come on,'
She cannot know the poignance of lapsed
purposes. Age – or deflected will?

The spirit of the garden ghosts by –
grey bearded, gaunt and pale
as the gum trees. Leaves might grow
from his finger tips. 'There's Santa,' she cries.
Perhaps, indeed, he brings her a gift –
for the future – of a cool, green place,
poised at the edge of myth or remembrance.

Sleeping

Half tipped on its side, between
weathered slabs – a robin. The tail
and a wing are spread wide,
a leg extended rigid to a claw
that might have tried to grip
the impossibly lubricated air.
The breast is flushed, a little ruffled –
though nothing to suggest panic. An eye
is already shrunk behind its glaze.

'Look, look,' she whispers, a finger
to her lips, 'a bird is sleeping in the grass.'
How to explain the inconceivable?
I carry her to the churchyard wall,
look over into the glen. We're above
a few dregs of cloud trailing
their smirr across the roof of the wood.
I explain about rain. But
behind me is a sleeping robin.

Encounter

'Bonjour. Je m'appelle Emily…'
Solemnly, she's addressing a toad
in her one morsel of French. What strange
impulse moves this three-year-old?
Bent by a forest track,
she's parting the glittering grasses
with a twig. Instinctive politeness?
A sort of reverence for a creature
whose world, she knows, is beyond
the limits of her understanding?

She gives her one resource –
disclosure of her precious name.
What power she offers in her innocence –
the single word that an ancient spell
might always have been prepared for.
And suddenly you see how a princess
might deserve her prince – that leap
into simple consideration.
But stubbornly brown and warty
he shuffles on. She skips away.

Oh child, child how can I carry
the burden of your wisdom?

Hallowe'en

Pale. Eyes ghosted. Usually
you skip from nursery, run
through the trees. I'm cold, you say,
and hold my hand. Your pirate top
is thin, your cap adrift.

I'd stitch for you a coat of leaves,
caught this moment as they twist
through gold October. Then I see
at your feet last winter's webs –
they'd hardly keep the wind away.

I'd cut a dress from sunlight
but it runs through fingers more slippery
than water. And where it's stopped
there are only shadows. You're wary
as they leap under an eager dog.

Starlight's too far to reach
and the moon, pale and unreliable.
Down sails by with the passing swans.
Mouse fur is too nimble. The meadow
keeps only memories of flowers.

I'll give you this – but, oh,
its difficult to see how words
will keep you warm. Except,
perhaps, once in a while, if
you remember, they'll make you smile.

Oregon Pine and a Child

It wasn't the spirit of place – for she ran,
happy and laughing by the spring wood,
brought something from the depths of a woman's
passing face that looked like joy.

It wasn't the wind, in its tiresome
insistence on recalling a passion of winter,
for in spite of itself, it shifted the hanging
larches to a shimmer of bright green.

It was more, perhaps, an instinctive
shiver at sublimity under a great pine,
the swart roots braced across rock
before knuckling into submissive earth.

And the cage of its trunks, like the limbs
of an ancient yew, stretched into dizziness,
promised some dire entrapment,
a dumb and wooden metamorphosis.

And its shadow – the nothing that is,
a bold, yet subtle absence –
whispered these intuitions of loss
that haunt even the happiest of children.

'No,' she said, 'I don't like it.' And ran.

Star Trail

While Tinker Bell
trailed stars across
the screen, she held
her biscuit, poised
for a bite. A minute, ten,
fifteen – until
she remembered.
Like waking. Slowly.

The hand crept.
Her world recovered.
Or was it something
less – a fall
into another sleep?
Pity the child
unhaunted by
a lost perfection.

V

Another Season

A sea, deep blue, cavorting,
running south, resolving to a swathe
of breaking sunlight. And Rum substantial
as a doubt, purple as the bloom of sloes,
its glens dove-grey, receding,
filled with silver light and slanting
rain. And above its troubled counter-
cloudscapes, the resonant sapphire bell.

Our boat is passing with its freight
of souls, lives wandering their alleys,
our small-town thoughts, preoccupations,
odd geographies and climates – no doubt,
familiar – warnings to trespassers,
high fences with their ambiguities
where keeping out is locking in –
our solitary, incommunicable worlds.

But, for a moment, we make a passage
to rock and sea and rain – we meet
beyond us, know something shared
that feels like flight in the company
of the sailing fulmars. And then the slow,
protracted loss. Except, we've touched
another season – elusive as a hint
of spring that draws us out of doors.

Chiaroscuro

Grey dogs shift over Eashaval –
they searched all night
for the absent moon. From a doubt
of sea or cloud the Atlantic
resolves to milky green.

For the sun breaks. Like a lost
child it's found its trail
in clues of machair flowers –
blue forget-me-not, corn
marigold, purple clover.

Perhaps summer nights
always brought marauders –
raids by the blind. They hurtle
past in cars. Their lager cans
lie buckled in a ditch.

Nearby, a dead otter
sleeked by the rain. Perfect –
though its teeth are bloodied.
It slips from stillness into
the mind – leaves a bright wake.

Sleepless

Uibhist a Deas,
            I saw you from Balranald,
I saw your hills
            and the sea, blue-black
and turquoise.
            I ran to the south,
                      as the sun
fell behind the machair
            I ran
to Cille Pheadair.

            And the base of the cloud
became the sweep
            of your shores,
                the piled
cloud your amethyst
            and purple mountains,
a Uist of the clouds
            set in a sea
of orange light,
          its reefs
            and archipelagos
in running gold.
            Time and the eye
stretched wide,
            stretched
                into the heart's
peace.

But in the night I cried
put away your beauty,
                              turn away
and let me sleep.
                    Oh mistress,
                                mistress –
when I close my eyes
                        they burn
                                with your light.

But the dawn is blessedly bleak,
                                confirms
you a creature of time.
                        Like the rest of us.

The Games at Ashkernish

Grim, they are, in their wee shelter
on the machair – the pibroch judges.
A cold wind flutters their papers.
A piper puffs and pummels, twists
his drones, then sooths his anguished
instrument. As a foot slides forward
he begins, stalking like an exotic heron.

Eyes drawn into his distance, the ascent
of his lonely mountain, you lose the crowd,
the bouncy castle, the denominational
tabernacles with their trestles of cakes,
a girl with her lucky prize of some
awful orange animal, a bunch
of merry youths with rasping hooters.

And that thin strand of lamentation
brings a different weave – pulse
of the Atlantic, soft plaid
of the machair, cry of the plover,
cadences of rock and sky.
But held in their knot, the stone men
never stir on their lonely mountain.

Gibbet

A lonely felon in a wide
landscape, a hoodie craw
hangs by the neck from a fence.
A pirate from Barra the crofter says.
His nearest neighbour is a lark
on a distant post. Even
the flies have had their fill.
Feathered rags and bones
turn slowly on the gibbet –
he seems to stir at the sight
of slate-black hills beaten
under dark wings of rain.
Then sunlight breaks
across the machair, lights
the stretch of houses straggling
through Cille Pheadair, lifts
all hints of prophecy
from a dangling bird.

Martha and Mary

For the Revd. Jackie Petrie

The white church at Howmore
is bold against an Atlantic sky,
stalwart in the authority of the Word.
Nearby, are ancient chapel gables
where the wind sings an old song.

A Viking princess was buried there.
Once a centre of learning, perhaps
their scriptorium looked out on Hecla,
Corrodale, Ben More, mountains
that lifted their eyes to their God.

I'll remember your Martha and Mary –
the way you caught us. We wait
to be surprised by the everyday –
busy Martha doing what she ought.
And Mary, lost in the Divine.

But its Martha who brings us closer.
The awkward business of living
once ebbed and flowed by these
weathered stones: service, you said,
sustained by vision – the reconciliation.

Strange the rhythms of time: the stretch
into shrouded distance; the sudden
compelling nearness. At sunset, we walk
the beach: north, on the wet sand's
fiery glitter; south, on penitential violet.

Summons

The bogs fissured, gripped
in drought. Then I found a gimmer,
stuck in a dub. The front legs
scrabbled at a bank. I straddled
and pulled behind the shoulders
but nothing stirred in the toothless
suck of the black maw.
Then like an ancient wrestler
from a story, I bent, and folded
round, and heaved. Still nothing
budged. Another heave stole
half a staggering step. The third,
a sweating deliverance. Or so
I thought. For though the front legs
kicked, the half of her lay
twisted, floundering in the heather.
What to do? Pass on.
I left her in that wilderness. I'd fought
with death. And he'd grinned and let
the matter drop. But as I walked
I heard him croak for his ravens.

Waiting for the Ferry

You wander through the drift of passengers,
note faces that in hours
that follow will grow intrusive,
too intensely familiar –
but the folk remain utterly unknown.

Through the brown-soup stir
in the lee of a wall, jut
the bones of a bike and a pale
plastic fish box.

White and blue and orange – strayed
from a Derain painting – a fishing boat
is restive on its tether. Creels
piled on the pier trawl the wind,
bequeath their fish-salt tang.

You imagine the drop to the gill-world,
and a crawling, armoured sentience
bearing its rhythmic burden
of the weight of tides, its aerials
thrumming to its water songs –
the scents of a lover, of a drifting
rancid morsel. It recoils
at a black-ghoul shadow, a twisting
cormorant; wonders at the comet tails
of bubble-wrapped gannets,
lethal angels plunging
through its firmament. From dumb rocks
it envies it neighbours lifting
through that fractured paradise of light.

The wind is throwing its weight about.
It pauses to consider.
We study the dubious sky
and wonder at our own passage.

VI

Above the North Esk

Tree in a clearing on a slab
of dawn. Its antlered limbs
are black. But edged in glittering
cinder-glow. Above the Esk,
tiers of oak and birch and beech
recede in pale-butter sunlight
that ignites the colour-chaos of decay.
A dialogue of crows echoes
in wood-smoke blue frost-haze.
And Hawthornden Castle
on its craig – as if built
for the picture. Time's sleight
of eye obscures its purpose.

Urgent along the ravine, a buzzard
side-slips, under-wings
flashing between the trees. It lifts
through a mobbing pair of jackdaws.

You wonder if his window's there.
Sir William must have known
this stepping out, this freedom.
And looking round lament
the folly of his fear of death –
which is, of course, our own.

And stepping out, you make
your magic circle and return.
Tree in a clearing – its light
extinguished. The frost-melt's cold
in dripping moss and lichens.

Autumn Spider

The spider in the bath
is stubborn. What drives him
up the glacial curve
to the point of losing traction?

He sees that walking upright
on the planet is perverse, condemns
to an infinite circularity –
how odd to live
with your head stuck in the blue,
to dangle upside down,
absorbed as a fly sucking
on a sugar-weeping apple.

In daring aerial experiments
he explores alternative perspectives
sustained by impossibly thin
ropes. Studies the obscenely
hairy, downcast human
crowns and the queer way
their limbs flick forwards.

His dream is to complete his arc
and walk upon the stars.

Vole

Two days you've lain
                       a perfect
moon-curve,
               the dark fur
of your back
               resolved to the pale
trail
    of your tail.
                  Your fore-feet
are knuckled
               more in petition
than any conceivable
                  threat,
your vole-blunt head
               bowed
in acceptance of the simple
                    wound
in your flank.

           Some
               cat-toy?
But the fur un-mouthed –
                  too
                     boring
in your final
           stillness?
                Where we
would stamp
               the boot of our
                   contempt
on something
           conquered.

Our crows
and magpie in its
burdened
flight
are not
deflected
and the fox
content
at loose in its winter
mortuary.

More
dead
than the
twitching
leaves –
and
your eye
an extinguished
star
fallen
through this bitter dusk
into a final
darkness.

February – Loch Ard

A pure symmetry of boathouses
casts a church window – murky
gold in the shadow. A goosander
threads the reflection, pauses
to consider his iconic exaltation.

Goldeneyes keep falling
through a door that seems
substantial. You plot the random
dimples of a little flock
that's never wholly present.

Together, suddenly, they lift
and hustle up the loch.
Their turbulence glazes,
permits the still goosander
to dream upon himself.

He's there and not there, stuck
in the varnish of an old master.
Bored with this perfection
he drives across the window.
It churns to silver in his wake.

Balloch

You wonder if they're glued –
the gulls on the ice. Stone-
still. In bare feet.
An impatient adolescent glances
over its shoulder, pads
three steps. Then sticks.

Out from the edge of their shelf
light glances, slides.
Posts of an old pier
are staggered like bad teeth,
their grizzled reflections chivvying
into grey. The ducks have lost
their dignity, jostle for crusts
thrown by a reluctant toddler.

A white boat is nudging
a fish-bone ripple. Slowly,
it's pushing towards sunlit,
snow-ridged mountains.

Lost to that inward eye
of winter, the gulls are lifting
on white-plumed peaks
that roar under the soaring albatross.

No-man

Something he cannot
                    understand,
some
        plague,
                perhaps out of the air,
is
    gnawing
            at his arms his
                        head.
Slowly,
        surely they
                    slump.
Where nose
            and eyes had been,
pits
        spread, decay
                    into the shadowed
undulations
            of a pale, glistening
moonscape.
                Does he know
                            terror
at his creeping
                oblivion?
                            This
unlikely articulation of
                        water –
does he fight,
                in dumb
struggle,
        his slow seeping
into the earth?

Soon he'll be
nothing.
What consolation is
a rumour
of resurrection
in Spring grass?

Snowman –
no-man.

VII

By La Poujade

Hunters only pass this way.
   The lane is overgrown.
A butterfly or two drop
   through a bitter weave –
no princess sleeps behind
   these barbs, the rampant
brambles. We've come for figs.
   But they're unreachable –
like the grail. There's something
   that no sword
encountered – a power-line
   looping through the flowers.

Derelict houses – you never
   see bits fall.
Perhaps they wait for storms.
   Discrete within
that turmoil, windows in their frames
   crash out.
And time has other agents –
   ivy, stealthy,
prising at the gutters, easing
   between bricks,
digesting mortar, till a heave
   of frost brings
landslides. Or is it passions
   that the walls absorbed,
left unconstrained by presences,
   destroying the substance
that they never had? And
   when we look,
they stop, transform themselves
   to innocent shadows.

Then looking back you see
   the hint of a roof,
and wonder, who, and why,
   what moment tipped
into abandonment, sent green
   resurgence sprawling
up the walls. Three trees
   are stark against the sky –
two sentinel poplars
   and a trunk of bone.

At Saint-Antonin-Noble-Val

Depths of sunlight where an eye might
drown, flow in the cobbled fissures
between shops and medieval houses.
By the river, shadows are cut tight
under the trees. They could be caves
into the underworld – steep, black,
depthless. Such an entrance drew
down Orpheus, daft in love.
And you hear of folk with ropes and helmets
compelled to return, squeeze into the womb.
But who would wish to try, to leave
this song of a day? On the far bank
half a dozen painters study the bridge.

It takes courage to commit to failure –
though you might just render enough
to persuade that here you'd lived for a morning.
At an exhibition of contemporary art
the rooms are full of whispers – for it's history
that speaks from galleries, the pang
of loss. Though now and then a moment
opens from a frame and lets you in.

Out in the heat, you pass a house
with cannily plundered corbels leering
from the walls and shrink, surprised as Alice,
to your mote of time. Then fall, sucked
through the familiar, past loss, into the fathomless.

For though suns rose, cats stalked
and nightingales sang, there's nothing stranger
than the worlds we dreamed into reality.
We kill for invisible gods. Imagine
walking into carnage, de Montfort's zealots
at their slaughter – and when you turn to look
you've lost the door from which you entered.

But we find our way through the press
of stone and time to an open space
where plane trees and the sun have reached
a shadowy accommodation. And drive away.

At Coylus

A tortoiseshell cat carries
its light-and-dark from heat
to shade across the Rue d'Eglise.

Agony, found in the wood,
hangs in the church from a hand
nailed to the north wall.
The writhe stretches, carved
from the twist of a single tree.
From where a branch was torn
the hole in the trunk is jagged.

The sculptor carved a carpenter,
his chisel marks, the signature
of artifice. But where He had roofed
a house, replaced a door-jamb –
blackened his thumb with a hammer –
his making merged into living.
They paid for his work to be invisible,
lost in purposes fulfilled.

In the cool under this wrought stone,
beauty is entrapment, demands
submission. Spirit – and power:
how close to the wind we sail.

But remember the thyme beneath
our feet, the celebrant cicadas,
and Notre-Dame-de-Grace
under a flawless sky? Below,
the Bonnette's wooded valley,
beyond, St-Pierre-Livron, a terraced,
hillside village, its orange
and ochre glittering in the sun.
It must be human insistence
to reach for grace through agony.
Those wise in love, let be,
wait for the full song.

Each careful foot – the cat
could be walking on cloud.
It wears the mark of all
eventualities, proceeds with dignity
towards its unknown purpose.

Afternoon

Caged by the heat
in orchard shadows,
you watch some wisps
of cloud un-strand,
re-wind in a slow
twist, dissolve.

A moment's breeze
stirs a grey exhalation
from a poplar.
Envy the wing-beat
draught from the dipping
butterflies.

A hoopoe lifts
into a feral apple tree,
raises his question,
folds into startling
light and shade. And
then – invisibility.

VIII

The Guidman's Daughter

Mary, Queen of Scots, was born at Linlithgow Palace on 8th December, 1542. And six days later, following the defeat of his army at Solway Moss, her father, James V, died at Falkland Palace. King James was known for wandering the country incognito and became popularly known as the Guidman of Ballingeich, the Red Tod – because of his auburn hair – and the Gaberlunzie Man – the wandering beggar.

The following September, Mary was crowned Queen at Stirling. Not quite six, she was sent to France where her mother, Marie de Guise, was highly connected. Mary's best friends accompanied her as maids of honour – the four Maries.

The regency of Marie de Guise was fraught with dynastic and religious conflict. At the end of 1543 the Scots had rescinded their recently arranged Treaties of Greenwich with England whereby Mary was to have been betrothed to Edward, Prince of Wales. By this marriage, his father Henry VIII had planned to unite the two kingdoms. Thwarted in his dynastic ambitions, in 1544 Henry launched an invasion which laid waste to southern Scotland – this appalling episode later came to be known as 'The Rough Wooing.' Apart from the terrible human suffering – inflicted as a matter of policy – irreplaceable buildings and artefacts of Scotland's Medieval and Renaissance culture were destroyed. The warfare was to last intermittently for seven years.

Further destruction followed the return from Geneva of John Knox in 1559. He preached a series of incendiary sermons, beginning in Perth. Protestant revolutionary zeal spread across the Central Lowlands resulting in the sacking and partial demolition of churches, monasteries and the great abbeys of Scone and Lindores.

Safe from this turmoil, Mary was brought up within the family of the King of France, Henry II, where she was a favourite. What a childhood this must have been at Chateau D'Amboise and the other royal residences, where the French Queen, Catherine de' Medici presided over the glittering entertainments. Catherine was the daughter of Lorenzo II de' Medici, ruler of Florence and Duke of Urbino.

Mary married the Dauphin in 1558. This reflected Henry's ambition to extend the power of France by incorporating Scotland into a larger empire. He also had his eye on Mary's claim to the English throne. The sickly Francis became King of France but died in 1560 leaving Mary as the Dowager Queen. She returned to rule her own kingdom in 1561. She was only nineteen. The magnificence of French courtly life behind her, you can but wonder what she thought as she landed in her small, grey kingdom at Leith, on a dreich day in August.

For a few brief years, even amidst the ideological maelstrom of the Reformation, she established a vibrant, Renaissance court – as both her father and grandfather had done. By celebrating Mass she put herself in bitter conflict with Knox but, nevertheless, held her kingdom together with tact and skill. The beginning of her end was in her marriage to the weak and debauched Henry, Lord Darnley. He was assassinated in mysterious circumstances in February 1567 while recovering from an illness, possibly syphilis. Henceforth, Mary's enemies would desperately try to implicate her in the murder.

Mary's situation rapidly deteriorated as a consequence of her subsequent marriage to James Hepburn, Earl of Bothwell, generally believed to have been the principal murderer of

Darnley. Ruthless and ambitious, he had allegedly abducted Mary and carried her off to his stronghold at Dunbar – he may have raped her. Three weeks later, she married him. He had, with extraordinary haste, arranged to have his wife, Jean Gordon, file a divorce petition.

The next month, at Carberry Hill, confronted by a confederation of rebellious lords, Mary's troops melted away. The rebels' opposition to Bothwell in his new position of power was greater than their loyalty to their Queen. Indeed, many Scottish nobles put the interests of their families before monarch and country.

It was the last time she was to see Bothwell. She negotiated his passage from the field while surrendering herself. Mary was imprisoned at Lochleven Castle. Five weeks later, as she lay recovering from a miscarriage, she was forced to sign away her crown to her infant son James, who would be raised as a Protestant.

Following her subsequent escape and defeat at Langside, she was imprisoned in England. Her relationship with Elizabeth had always been difficult – compounded by the machinations of Elizabeth's chief advisor, William Cecil, Lord Burghley.

Eventually, after eighteen years of confinement, in desperation Mary became involved in the Babington Plot, a conspiracy that would have involved the assassination of Elizabeth. On 1st February, 1587, Elizabeth signed her death warrant and on 8th February, Mary was executed at Fotheringhay Castle. At forty-four, crippled by arthritis, this intelligent, beautiful, compelling woman could hardly walk to the scaffold.

At Stirling Castle

September, 1543

The Guidman of Ballingeich –
you imagine, of a night, he'd slip
down the brae, wander
the town. Be kind to beggars.
And what's Marie of Guise
to a night of houghmagandy?
One of God's appointed.
And the Solway Moss enriched
by blood and bone. Does
he die of the flux – or despair?

Fortress, palace – prison?
They barred the windows to protect
their infant queen. Of an afternoon
she'd see the slow sweep
of shadows along the tapestries,
her wee hand reaching
for light as their stories passed
into the dusk. In the Chapel Royal
a crown is held over her head.
Then she falls in a whimpering sleep.

After the feast, the masques –
a swirl of dancing. They stotter
into the dark. Glow of embers
in the Great Hall. Acrid ghosts
stretch across the roof. Cold
wood smoke. Moonlight lies
with the dogs under the High Table.
And the slow weight
of that anointing – it gathers
like snow, its ice inexorable.

Leith

19th August, 1561

She dreams of drownings. Takes root
on the poop deck. Her eyes are restive
over textures of grey, her royal pennons
shrouded. Smoke on the breeze? The sudden
pier looms, bulking through ambiguity.
And this, her inheritance? She twists
from the grip of loss. Adieu, la France…
Adieu…. And her Francois dead. August –
but the chill bleaches even beneath her pallor.

They ride from empty Leith. And catch
her palace – insubstantial, adrift
like her ship in a tide of drizzling wraiths.
Uncanny, like something at the edge
of thought she cannot read. But the sun
breaks – and her father's keep resolves
to stone. Her eyes are searching for warmth
in doubtful smiles. Crowds gather.
Her hope and trust is in hearts.

Remembering Orléans

April, 1565

In the shadow of a crow, she'd seen
how the soul might take flight
for the House of Death. But knew,
at the bottom of her mind,
she could never be Andromache, wild
on the ramparts bewailing her Hector.

Fellowship, a brother, their kingdom
of childhood lost – but no song
for Aphrodite. L'amour courtois –
in her child's heart, its fictions
had rooted, flourished in love's
gestures, its giddy ritual.

She'd wept for her shilpit laddie –
and woke to a winter season,
to a loss the more bitter for what
they'd never had. Now she prays
for a glimpse of love's divinity.
And finds a beautiful boy.

At Holyroodhouse

March, 1566

I'd like to believe you weren't lost
in the myth of yourself. I can see you
dancing your widow's shadow away,
teasing the Maries, waving your cape
at the snorting Knox, tally-ho-hunting
Moray in a steel cap with your pair
of pistols – playing chess with another
canny queen. I climb to your apartments
up the back stair, sidle with other
tourists through your bedroom – strange,
what time arranges. Was it here you played
that other game, mistress of prevarication,
countering the drunken, poxy Darnley?

A March evening. Supper spread,
a fire in the grate, though its flame
is frail across walls replete in their store
of winter darkness. And nightmare
breaks in a storm-surge. The table
crashes and Riccio's screams buoyant
above the welter. A pistol at your head,
hunched, you wrap your arms tight
across your womb for the child
that will never be yours. The tide swirls
through your rooms beneath Ruthven's harangue –
Yir tyranny, madame, wi cannae thole....

Words drain into the dark. You stand
ghost-pale in the wreckage of a storm-beach.
Then silence. Unbelievable silence.
It feeds the mind's riot. And your Oratory
unreachable across the stained floor.
You rock and shiver through that night –
the Fontainebleau darling, their little Queen.

At Craigmillar

November, 1566

Folk enter between yews grown crooked
to catch the light, climb through the weight
of stone to view that hill-top town
on the sky-line – so small. She would see it
at sunset in conflagration – the fortress
on its rock, St Giles stark against flame.

A melancholy queen. In dreams she twists
from the breath of black-mouthed shadows.
Remembers steel arcing through firelight.
But Jamie safe in Stirling. Takes refuge here,
where she'd been happy. But in the dark,
the walls are whispering stories of conspiracy.

Haar flows round the tower house.
Obscures the sky. But out on the hill
her falcon would fly, is restive on her wrist,
tears at the stain on her fist. She finds
a rag of blue – lifts her to the sun.
Forgets the terrible exposure of the dove.

At Dunbar

April, 1567

And the stoor still settling
over Darnley. As she reached
that Almond brig, was she dreaming
of Notre-Dame, a glittering white
and blue Dauphine? Bothwell's
quarry – his dogs unleashed.
A *rash and hazardous young man.*

Did she think to tame him –
chain him to a pomegranate tree,
her unicorn? And the bristled boar
loose, rooting in her garden.

That witchcraft she knows fine
well. Knows exactly
what she does. But the delusion –
his power for her – can't she see
its promise is frail as a breath?
Exhausted by constraint she throws
the last of her youth at a venture.

April – wakes to the cry
of gulls on an east wind.
And Jean, his wife, Jean
Gordon? Risen from their bed,
she stands on a rampart, looks
north into her kingdom, remembers
the penitential season. Pebbles
rattle in the waves' throats;
kittiwakes are flying seaward
into the dawn's furnace.

Carberry Hill

June, 1567

Rituals of love and battle – how they clung
to the old dispensation, its theatricality.
They danced their darkness to the choreography
of chivalry. But a dress rehearsal – with never
a death. Though the young crows waited,
ragged in the trees. But hot from their hill,
in the June sun, wearied, parched on wine,
her army was drifting back to Edinburgh.

What desperate loyalty tied her
after brutal nights, the anguish that reached
the Maries through the bristling dark?
And her pale face drawn and runnelled.
Perhaps the knot she carried in her womb?
She watched the dust of Bothwell's
urgent passage stain the distance.

Slowly, she rode to Carberry Tower –
to something new. The cat-calls grew
in that strange release from dead authority.
And they looked away, her confederate,
rebel Lords, as she stood in scarlet –
her borrowed clothes – expecting
to be helped. Little more than a girl –
did she see that her life was already lived?
Murtherin' bitch, the Roman whoor.

At Lochleven Castle

June, 1567 – May, 1568

A warm south wind –
and a smoke of gnats warps
in the lee of keep and trees.
Black pennons. She brought
her shadows to this dark house.
In sweat and cries, miscarries
twins. And her dreams return
to that moment – the pale, upturned
faces – where she stands, distraught,
half-naked in the provost's
window above the Mercat Cross,
while folk gather, bewildered,
murmuring – their captive Queen.

And then, at prayer, she sees
her pieces falling into the picture.

Slowly, she wakes to summer,
doos crooning down the chimneys,
arrives at sunlight and the grace
of swallows, the dance of water
and the saugh of reeds. Runs
with the corn flowing in distant
fields, and her foot tapping
to an old song as she stitches
the white rose. But she knows
that to fly, swans must
learn to walk on water.

And the screw turns. Was it just,
in the end, she was a woman?
You can see, any night, our
crushing Scot's brutalities,
the blood and glass. And you hear
the blast of that Trumpet - a woman's
rule, *is repugnant to nature,*
contrary to God. She signs
the papers, and the crown passes
to a bairn whom Buchanan would teach
to despise his idolatrous mother.

Sheffield

1570 – 1582 at various times

She remembers how her hands
betrayed her – the washerwoman
with flashing eyes –
their marble elegance.

Quietly, they pull her
back to the island – hands,
that are easy round the oars,
hairy, over broken nails.

A neep with a bunnet –
not without humour –
but a man who knows his duty.
If not to his queen.

Then Willie Douglas,
starry-eyed, she seduced
with stories – life,
love and chivalry

in foreign courts.
In the dirl and thump
of swaggering reels,
he steals his faither's keys

and out they glide
past a squawking heron
on a treacherous quiet
thick with mayflies.

And then at Langside,
that Stuart talent – defeat
from likely victory.
And a long, long road.

She wanders her regal
apartments, plays her lute,
talks to her caged birds.
Weeps for the Phoenix:

En ma fin est mon commencement.

Chartley

1586

Time
and circumstance make
their moves –
a white
or a black queen?

Who was
this woman – compelling,
passionate? Would
she have been happy,
born without a crown?

She watches the tremors
in a web
spun
across her window.

The moon
might be
at the bottom of a well.

And her wee man –
so far, so
long
out of reach.

She sweeps the shadows
from her mirror.
Studies
a spirit,
confined,
that is breaking her body.

And her boy,
who couldn't remember her,
his eye on crowns
would consign her
to inconsequence –
mother of the King.

my deluded son.

In the light of dawning
a web
is steely
across her window.

A spirit,
confined,
is breaking her mind.

She falls, falls,
reckless in despair.

At Fotheringhay

February, 1587

Spent chestnut flowers, flooding
  the gutters. Hawthorns swaying,
heavy in fretted lace. Your looking
  is careful, as if you half
expected some hint encrypted in the day
  to open and disclose an anguish,
a tremor at the root or in the enigmatic
  mirror of the Nene. But
nothing speaks except tranquillity.

*

They brought her in September.
She watched the mists drift trees
  along slow horizons,
lost herself in October's amber afternoons,
  its bitter-sweet deceptions,
saw parables in light and water, the abyss
  descend beyond the edge
of comforting reflections. Each dusk
  drew her further into the dark.
Cold passed like spirit through the stone,
  settled in more vulnerable bone,
took shapes in sleep that stretched
  into the gestures of the proximate dead.
Waking, she'd sail free on the gold
  and scarlet of winter mornings,
foundering in the lapse to a grey day.
  Bowed, on her knees, did she read
that prophetic gesture as she breathed the ash
  of penitence to a cold flame –
and reached at joy? Held tight
  in that knot of circumstance,

her dignity defiant, she wrested her meaning
from a stubborn February dawn.

That endless, fleeting night, elusive
as the scent of flowers, she'd touched
on moments of serenity, drifted in Carver's
silver labyrinth – *O good Jesus…*
O sweet Jesus…

And the edge
            falls.
                    Between
                            word
and word.
            As jackdaws
                    racket
in spare chestnuts.
                    And hands
                            are drenched
that help her hold
                    her crucifix.

It falls.
            Between night and night.
As a body
            dances its mandatory figures.
As a river fills
            with light.

It falls.

As kites, forked
on the wind,
swoop
at gobbets on the midden.

Witnesses
grip their souls
as a white
cropped head
continues
to mouth
unintelligible mysteries.

At Falkland Palace

2008

Red Tod's lassie – a girl
who'd wear breeches at tennis
or skelping after deer hounds.
You can see the frozen faces,
black affrontit. She'd climb
to the priest's room. The stones
are worn as if by tides. You might
be walking on her shadow.
He'd sit, crow black,
under the dazzle from his window.
Bless me, Father, for I have sinned.

Fingers pressed together,
behind the venialities, he'd imagine
her circle of Hell. Did he find,
by that light in her face, few
sins of intention? But animal spirits,
tied down by the jesses? Perplexed,
he'd see how our strengths can destroy us.
And late the struggle to be wise.
He remembers her tawny eyes,
and the Maries capering, their laughter
ringing in the winter courtyard.

It cam' wi a lass and it will gang
wi a lass. Then he turned his face
to the wall. Only the wind sings
in Knox's rubble; round gables,
blackened from a Rough Wooing.
In that February dawn old Scotland
limps away. She carries our
language in the wallet on her back.
A sad tale for the Gaberlunzie Man.